Agile Testing:

An Overview

By

Florian Heuer

Contents

Introduction

Software testing can often be a slow procedure, especially when it's carried out following traditional business principles. Scheduled meetings, deadlines for the next version to be discussed and the need for every department to sign off on results impose endless delays and make it hard to get a product deployed before it's already obsolete. It's very frustrating, which is why more and more developers are turning to methods that go by the promising name of *Agile*.

The word *agile* implies speed, flexibility and creative freedom, so it's sometimes applied to any less structured way of doing things, but when it comes to software development it usually refers to a specific process outlined in the *Agile Manifesto*. This was put together in 2001 by a group of software engineers frustrated by the outdated procedures being followed in their companies. Seventeen people gathered in a ski lodge in Snowbird, Utah, to rewrite the rules of their industry. In the software development community their conference has taken on an almost legendary status, and their philosophy is now widely followed.

The 68-page *Agile Manifesto* is a set of principles geared at improving the development process. Drawn from a variety of workflow systems – Scrum, Lean, Kanban, XP and others – it filtered out the most valuable techniques and assembled them into a way of thinking that encourages fast, adaptable design. They summed it up in a brief statement:

Manifesto for Agile Software Development

We are uncovering better ways of developing software by doing it and helping others do it. Through this work we have come to value:

Individuals and interactions *over processes and tools*
Working software *over comprehensive documentation*
Customer collaboration *over contract negotiation*
Responding to change *over following a plan*

That is, while there is value in the items on the right, we value the items on the left more.

That statement sums up the basics of Agile – it's focused on goals instead of processes. It aims at flexibility and responsiveness. It doesn't ask you to do things for the sake of doing them, but focuses on delivering an end product. It's all about getting the software you want, not the software the process delivers.

Agile sounds like a great idea, but implementing it can put many people off.

Traditional software design processes are based on tried and tested procedures imported from manufacturing industries. They're not tailored for the very different processes involved in developing software, but they do work and their familiarity is reassuring to management. To do Agile properly means a radically different way of working and for many the step into the unknown is intimidating. It means breaking down the boundaries between developers and testers, forging new connections across teams and abandoning a lot of the documentation and checklists that usually go along with the design process. Instead of teams handing the product back and forth as it proceeds through a series of carefully laid out steps the workflow is far more collaborative and dynamic. To traditional engineers Agile seems to throw out most of the quality safeguards they rely on, but in fact it replaces them with a whole new set that are far more likely to identify issues before they threaten the project.

If you think it's difficult to convince engineers it can be a lot harder to persuade senior management that switching to a radically different development system is a good idea. Many companies – especially large ones – are resistant to change, and Agile tends to involve a lot of change. The lack of detailed up-front planning makes people nervous when large budgets or key business capabilities are at stake, and the fluidity of task allocation and responsibility might look like a threat to some people's positions. These concerns usually aren't a genuine argument against Agile, though; most of the time they come from a lack of understanding, and once people have a grasp on how Agile really works they're generally a lot more enthusiastic.

If you want the benefits of Agile testing, but you're unsure of how to go about implementing it in your own business, then this book is for you. Inside you'll find a clear explanation of how Agile works, all you need to know about its principles and how to make it work for you. We give you real world examples plus information about some of the potential pitfalls and how to avoid them. By the time you've finished you'll know how to get started, what to expect and how to keep everything efficient, trouble-free and above all *Agile*. Remember:

Agile isn't something you *do*. It's something you *are*.

How Does Agile Testing Work? – Understanding The System

Before implementing Agile testing it's vital to know exactly what it is and how it works. Failure to understand this is the most frequent cause of unsuccessful experiments with Agile. It's understandable because it *is* a radically different way of working, but you're aiming for success and that means doing your homework before starting the switch. If you try to change over without knowing exactly what needs to be changed you're going to run into problems. First let's look at how things have traditionally been done, and why that way doesn't always work.

The Linear Approach

As software companies grew in the late 1970s and early 80s most of them adopted the familiar development process used by traditional engineering companies. That made sense at the time because there weren't any other reliable ways of developing a complex product, so they picked up a tool that worked. Often called the "waterfall" method, this is a linear process with a number of clearly defined steps:

9

- Requirements – The customer submits their list of requirements for the software, outlining what they need it to do.

- Design – The software architecture is designed from the requirements.

- Implementation – At this stage the code is written, following the architecture design.

- Verification – The software is tested to make sure it's stable and does what the customer wants it to do.

- Maintenance – Any issues with the software are corrected.

- Delivery – The final. Working software is delivered to the customer.

In practice the software often moves between the last three stages several times as issues are identified and resolved. Every time this happens delays are likely to occur. The main reason for delays is that developers and testers are set up as separate groups at different stages of the production cycle; every time the software is changed, or an issue is identified, it moves between the groups. Because what should happen at each stage of the process is clearly defined the developers are always aiming to deliver a perfect piece of code to the testers. A lot of time is spent making sure what goes to testing is as close to perfect as they can make it. The testers, in turn, are looking to identity every bug in the software and generate a comprehensive fault list to send back. More time disappears as the software is exhaustively scrutinized for every tiny defect.

The waterfall method is tried and tested and has been successfully used by engineers for decades. There are times when it will give good results. If your job fits the following criteria, it's likely to be a suitable choice:

- Requirements are well known, clear and unlikely to change
- The product definition is stable
- The technology is understood
- All required resources are freely available
- The project is short

On the other hand, if those conditions aren't met there are clear disadvantages. Here are the main ones:

- Once an application reaches the testing stage it is very difficult to go back and change anything that wasn't well thought through at the concept stage.

- No working software will be produced until late in the life cycle.
- High levels of risk and uncertainty are involved.
- Not suitable for complex and object-oriented projects.
- Not a good option for long or ongoing projects.
- Not suitable for projects where there is a moderate to high risk of changing requirements.

Before beginning a project it's vital to assess how you expect it to develop throughout its life cycle. If the criteria for waterfall development are met, it's fine to proceed using that method. Otherwise it's best to look for an alternative.

The Agile Alternative

Agile testing aims to eliminate the inefficient gap between development and testing. In effect the two functions are unified into a single process. That doesn't have to mean the same people do both, but the gap between the development and testing teams is removed and their functions are no longer separate stages of the process. Instead they're in constant contact with each other, so both development and testing run in parallel. Many organizations set up multifunctional teams that include both developers and testers; others have the coders run automated tests on their own and each other's work.

There are multiple benefits to this. Firstly, it saves time; instead of testers waiting until a finished product is delivered to them then beginning their evaluation, they can test constantly. As well as reducing down time this lets them identify potential issues early and flag them up to the developers, who can fix them there and then before too much effort has been invested in the wrong direction. It's a way of combining the strengths of both groups in a march towards a common goal, whereas under the traditional process they can seem more like adversaries constantly trying to outwit each other. It's the difference between saying "You did that wrong; try again" and "I think I can see a better way for us to do this." The result is faster, more integrated product development and a working piece of software that's delivered sooner and with fewer false starts. Linear development usually gets there in the end but a lot of time, money and effort can be wasted before that happens.

The key to Agile is that the workflow is much less rigidly defined. That doesn't mean it's anarchy, of course – Agile teams don't just start coding whatever everyone feels like, and each methodology has its own system for allocating tasks. It does move away from the step-by-step paradigm though. With the development and testing staff working closely together the emphasis moves from completing each clearly defined stage of the process to doing whatever is required right now to advance the project.

The concept of Agile can be hard to grasp at first glance, but broken down into its component parts it becomes much easier to understand. Here are the key principles of Agile testing:

- **Cooperative** – Developers and testers constantly work together towards a common goal – a finished piece of software

- **Non-Linear** – There are no stages to be passed through; all activity is development-focused.

- **Streamlined** – Effort isn't diverted into producing extensive documentation of what's being done; the team does what's necessary then documents what they've produced.

- **Adaptable** – Agile can swiftly cope with changes in customer requirements or new technological developments.

- **Transparent** – Information isn't stovepiped within separate teams – everything

14

everyone needs to know to complete the project is freely shared.

Of course that doesn't mean that Agile is disorganized. Far from it, in fact – activity is mapped out. The difference is the way that's done, and you have a choice of how to do it.

Agile itself is a set of principles. To implement it those principles should be used together with an suitable development framework. There are several of these, each of them with particular strengths. Choosing the right framework for your project will unlock the potential of the Agile principles. Here are some of the leading ones.

Scrum

Scrum aims to rapidly deliver working software then add to the feature set incrementally. The Product Owner develops a list of features ranked in order of priority, which is called the Product Backlog. This is used to plan development cycles, called Sprints. Each Sprint aims to deliver a subset of the product features, listed in the Sprint Backlog.

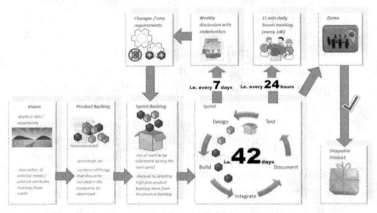

(see http://www.agile-testing.com/ebook-illustrations for a higher resolution)

Sprints usually last one to three weeks and integrate development and testing throughout. A bug-tracking system is used to list all defects and time is built into the Sprint schedule to fix them. Any defects found by the client after the iteration is delivered are added to the fix list for the next Sprint. Feedback about that iteration is also included in the task list for the next one.

Once the entire Product Backlog has been worked through the client receives the final version of the software. Any remaining defects are corrected on-demand at this stage, and once the Product Owner is satisfied they accept the completed project.

One of the key advantages of Scrum is that it recognizes how often customer requirements change in the course of a project. The incremental system breaks projects down into manageable tasks, and the aim is that each increment will deliver a product that's functional, fully tested and could be shipped if required. In most cases it won't be shipped immediately but where the client needs basic functionality as soon as possible, with more features added later, Scrum is tailor made to deliver that. On the other hand the Scrum framework doesn't cover the entire product development life cycle; for example it has no way to handle requirements gathering or high level design. For this reason it's common to use another methodology to handle this stage of the project then move to Scrum when development begins.

Scrum certification is available from Scrum Alliance and Scrum.org; these organizations will certify team members in general proficiency with Scrum as well as in specialist tasks such as Product Owner and Scrum Master. Certification can be useful in persuading management that Scrum is a useful development method.

Kanban

Kanban started out as a scheduling system built around lean, just-in-time principles before being adopted for Agile development. Originally developed by Toyota in the 1940s for traditional engineering tasks, it's managed the transition to software development very well. Kanban is similar to Scrum in that it breaks down the project into subsets, but there are also many differences. It's not an iterative approach to Agile. Instead, the task list is laid out on a special board known as a Kanban Board – *Kanban* is Japanese for "signboard" - that shows the current state of the project:

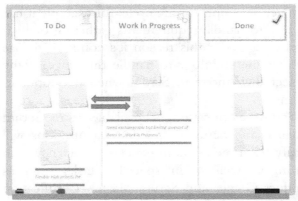

(see http://www.agile-testing.com/ebook-illustrations for a higher resolution)

The key to Kanban's agility is limiting the number of tasks in progress at any one time. This allows the team to identify and fix issues with each task and move them into the "Done" column, then begin work on a new set of tasks from the Backlog. Kanban is especially useful where tasks are changing often and there is no way to define a usable iteration. It's also a flexible system – rules and practices from other methods, including Scrum, can be added where required. Kanban itself has six basic principles:

1.   **Visualize** – Graphic displays are a key part of Kanban, allowing teams to easily check progress

2.   **Limit work in progress** – Tasks should be begun when needed, using a pull system

3.   **Manage workflow** – Moves of tasks between columns is tracked and recorded

4.   **Make policies explicit** – Everyone should understand how things are done

5.   **Implement feedback loops** – Review progress and issues constantly so the process can be refined

6.   Improve   collaboratively,   evolve experimentally

Like Scrum, Kanban is able to deliver working software early in the project then add functionality in increments. Based on the customer's priorities the core functionality is moved into the Work in Progress column first, and when it's moved to the Done column it can be shipped; the team can then move on to developing additional features to be included in the next release.

Kanban has been adopted by major software developers including Corbis and Microsoft. In fact Microsoft don't just use it for their own development; they now offer Kanban tools in their Dynamics products and even in OneNote

Scrum-ban

As the name implies this is a hybrid of features from both Scrum and Kanban. It's ideally suited for maintenance or update projects, where unexpected issues have to be resolved but Sprints are of little value. It's also a useful tool where you're using Scrum but having difficulty in delivering working software on time at the end of Sprints – introducing Kanban principles can help with reallocating resources and keeping the number of in-progress tasks down to a manageable level. It can be as simple as using a Kanban board to place a fixed limit on the number of user stories being developed in each Sprint – a metric that has a seemingly irresistible urge to grow.

Scrum-ban isn't a tightly defined system, mostly because it's new, but the basics are using

Scrum meetings in combination with Kanban's continuous workflow and task board.

XP

XP, or eXtreme Programming, is based around a set of practices that can be applied as and when needed – it's not always appropriate to use all of them. Key elements of XP include:

- Coding standards
- Refactoring (an evolutionary approach to software design)
- Unit testing
- Continuous integration – merging all working copies into a single "mainline" copy several times a day

Coding standards and refactoring are used in most projects. Unit testing and continuous integration are usually used for larger ones. XP makes heavy use of concepts like pair programming, test-driven development and simplicity of design.

XP is an iterative system, like Scrum, but doesn't use an overarching process framework to guide development. It has a stronger focus on engineering. Many teams use Scrum as their main development process but add elements of XP to overcome specific roadblocks.

Like Scrum, XP allows for a very flexible response to changing customer requirements. It emphasizes allowing the customer to request changes informally instead of going through a defined change request process, which allows for a faster response with less administrative overhead.

A Guiding Philosophy

Agile development isn't just a single system. It's a philosophical approach to writing software, and it offers a lot of choice in how you go about a project. Each of the popular Agile methods – there are more than the ones described here – has its devoted fans. They all have some things in common though. When you're planning the move to Agile always stay focused on achieving the core principles outlined in the Agile Manifesto:

• Aim for customer satisfaction through early delivery

• Welcome changing requirements

• Frequent software delivery

• Daily collaboration

• Build projects round motivated individuals – then support them

- Maintain face-to-face communication
- Measure progress by working software
- Set a sustainable pace
- Stay focused on technical excellence and good design
- Aim for simplicity and economy of effort
- Allow teams to self-organize – this gives the best results
- Regularly review your effectiveness and adjust as required

Identifying The Objective

It's fairly obvious that before beginning a project the development team need to know what the objective of that project is. Unfortunately this can be more difficult than it first seems, and a major cause of project delays is a failure to set the right objectives before work begins. Once that happens it's going to cost time and probably money to fix things at a later stage of development.

Following traditional methodology, the standard practice is to define as many requirements as possible up front. This can be very effective in the right circumstances. If your project meets all of the following criteria a detailed statement of requirements might be a good place to start from:

- Requirements are clearly understood
- All functionality can be met with mature technology
- Requirements are unlikely to change

Unfortunately while this is a good approach to designing a ship, when it comes to software development the situation is usually very different. Requirements change frequently, standards and available technology move on during the development process and the details of what the software actually needs to do may not be obvious at the beginning of the process. Serial design processes often deliver very inefficient results; lack of user testing means up to 64 per cent of the functionality that's delivered is rarely or never used. Very often it's excessive up-front modelling, and a fear of making changes later in the process, that generates this unnecessary functionality – the team set out to cover every possible contingency at the start, and these contingencies gradually get absorbed into the core of the project and delivered in the final build whether the customer actually needs them or not.

Because Agile is a less linear way of working, there is less emphasis on exhaustive planning at the start of the project. That doesn't mean the planning doesn't happen, but it does shift much of it to later stages in the cycle. The basic principle of identifying objectives in Agile is the same as the one that underlies testing – it's a continuous process, not a fixed stage. If you spend time at the beginning on writing detailed requirements that work will be wasted if the requirements change. It's far better to spend time on making sure the code can be tested as it's developed.

Instead, Agile developers aim to identify the bare minimum needed to get the project under way. The basic idea is that if you can identify detailed requirements before the project starts you can identify them even better when they're actually needed. This ties in well with iterative systems like Scrum and XP; requirements can be developed for each iteration rather than trying to work out everything that's needed for the entire project. That reduces the up-front project envisioning effort from weeks to days. At first glance it seems as if the work is just shifted downstream, but in fact developing a small batch of requirements is a task that's easily accomplished as part of the standard Scrum planning, whereas working out a full set inevitably becomes a major development stage of its own.

A good example of this approach is Agile Model Driven Development (AMDD). Model Driven Development is often used in waterfall development and relies on extensive modeling before coding starts. AMDD modifies it to suit Agile principles. This moves the bulk of the activity to product iterations and breaks it down into manageable, just in time tasks. By doing this there's no risk of investing time and effort in developing requirements that might change once the customer has seen early builds of the software.

Iteration 0

At this stage, usually during the first week of the project, the basic framework is worked out. A broad-brush approach is used rather than a highly detailed one, with the goal being to work out the high-level scope, initial requirements and the overall architecture to be used. Here is a typical Iteration 0 checklist:

• Is the testing environment ready? Do we have all the hardware and licenses we need?

• Do we have enough on the Project Backlog to support the first iterations?

• Does the team have all the required skills, or do we need to recruit?

• Is any training necessary before testing and coding begins?

Scrum doesn't lay down any processes for how to carry out Iteration 0, so elements of another system are usually brought in for this stage. Kanban methodology may be adopted, or a more traditional process similar to the waterfall method but without the focus on detailed planning and documentation. We'll look at that in more detail later, in the context of a SAP ERP implementation, under hybrid systems.

Subsequent Iterations

For each iteration of the project – corresponding to a sprint in Scrum or (roughly) to a refreshing of the Work In Progress list in Kanban – a new cycle of modelling is carried out. The modelling needs to be detailed enough to give good time and resource estimates for that iteration and plan the work involved. It doesn't go beyond immediate needs though – if you've generated the requirements for what the team is about to start on that's enough for now. You can always return to the model later if it needs more work. Again this means you won't waste time modeling something that doesn't make it to the final build.

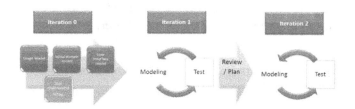

(see http://www.agile-testing.com/ebook-illustrations for a higher resolution)

Three elements usually need to be worked out in Iteration 0; while much less than in the traditional process these will give enough information to get started:

1.   Usage Model – The exact form of this depends on the Agile system you're using. Typical examples are a collection of essential use cases, features or user stories.

2.   Initial domain model – This identifies the entities who will use or be affected by the software and how they relate to each other.

3.   User interface model – A rough concept of how the users will interact with the software. This can include screen sketches or a prototype interface.

None of these elements needs to be developed in much detail – just enough to get the ball rolling on Iteration 1. More detailed objectives and components can be identified then.

Testing

Where the real detail is required at this stage is in planning the testing environment and beginning to set it up. Because most of the testing in Agile is carried out as a continuous process, not a discrete stage later in the development cycle, the testing strategy needs to be clearly understood right from the beginning. Factors to consider include:

- Implementation of Test Driven Development. TDD uses continuous testing as an aid to refining requirements; testing code is written *first*, designed to replicate what the user needs from the software, then operational code is written until the test is passed. This is the standard model in Agile development.

- Whole-Team testing or independent test team. Whole-team testing is effective for simpler projects where a single team is working, but at a large scale it becomes difficult to manage. Where multiple teams are working in parallel an independent test team can support multiple development teams.

- Testing environment setup. All the required testing tools should be in place at the start of the project. This includes hardware, software and the bug tracking system.

In an Agile development environment the initial stage of a project should prioritize getting ready to test over exhaustively working out the coding requirements. Requirements inevitably change as the project unfolds; the need for fast, responsive and appropriate testing does not. The vision of the software that will be developed can be sketched out roughly then refined later as actual requirements become clearer.

Identify Stakeholders

One of the key advantages of Agile development is the way it brings stakeholders and developers together during the process. Stakeholders are anyone who will be affected by the software; they include users, but also managers, operations staff, project funders, help desk staff, auditors and maintenance teams.

Why is stakeholder involvement important? It boils down to efficiency. It's difficult to provide a list of requirements that really describes what you're looking for, so when the customer provides a detailed specification then waits for delivery the final product isn't likely to exactly match what they want. This is where most unnecessary functionality is generated. It's also a major source of delay; if finished software meets the stated requirements, but not the actual ones, remedial work is going to be required. Changing stakeholder requirements are also an issue. It's not uncommon for the final product to match what the stakeholder wanted at one point in the process – usually an early one – but be significantly different from what they want *now*. A serial development process significantly increases the risk of this; very often stakeholders will sign off on the initial requirements then not see the software again until they're asked to carry out acceptance testing. By that point adding or altering functionality is likely to cause substantial delays and cost inflation.

By bringing stakeholders in at the start of the development process, and keeping them involved, it's much easier to keep the team's activity and the stakeholders' real requirements aligned. The final end users will have the chance to see each new component as soon as it's developed and give feedback. This has several advantages:

- Stakeholders will be able to quickly identify any mismatch between what they thought they wanted and what they really want.
- Missing functionality will be noticed early and can be added without major rewrites.
- Unnecessary functionality can also be identified (it won't get used) before much time has been wasted on developing it.

From the point of view of testing there are also clear benefits. The main one is a reduced load at the acceptance testing stage; by the time working software is delivered to the customer the end users already have extensive hands-on experience with development versions of it. They know it delivers the functionality they require, because if it didn't they would have made that known to the developers and it would have been fixed, so acceptance testing will usually be limited to finding any remaining bugs and checking compatibility with other systems.

Vision

Before work can start on the project you need to have a clear vision of what you're looking to deliver. The work done up to this point has been directed towards finding out what the stakeholders need. That's likely to add up to a lot of information, some of it perhaps contradictory. The key to building the vision is to sort through it all and come up with the outline of a product that will meet as many of the requirements as possible. That's going to need the involvement of stakeholders to resolve any questions and avoid misunderstandings, but the final result should be a clear statement, agreed on by everyone, of what exactly the finished software will do. The next stage is to start from there and work backwards to decide exactly what needs done to achieve the goal.

At this point it's easy to get bogged down in details. Resist the temptation. If you start to focus on small stuff you'll end up doing a lot of work that really isn't any more than speculation; at this stage you don't know enough about how the development will go to be looking at details. It's also easy to start channeling yourself towards decisions, where you might have ended up doing things differently if you'd left yourself enough freedom. Detailed planning also generates documentation, and that's far from the best way to keep up a good flow of information within your team and between the team and the stakeholders. In fact it's likely to lead to misunderstandings and a failure to get everyone headed for the same destination. Rather than rely on documentation to share information it's better to have people talking to each other directly.

There are a few key points you need to stay in control of during this phase of the project. They might seem obvious but it's amazing how often they get overlooked – Agile gives you a better chance of getting them right:

•   **What exactly does the stakeholder need?** With waterfall processes it's too easy for a disconnect to creep in between what the customer is looking for and what you think they're looking for – or, even worse, what you think they *should* be looking for.

•   **How are you going to achieve that?** This isn't a detailed plan of the work you intend to do; it's a general overview of how you're going to deliver the right functionality. As well as the customer's requirements you need to be informed by:

•   **Is it something you can build?** This is why you need to work backwards from the required product to the way you're going to produce it. If it turns out the stakeholders are looking for something you can't deliver this approach will identify the problem at an early stage, so you can work with them to come up with an alternative that meets their goals and which you *can* deliver.

Even at this stage the Agile technique you're planning to use will influence your work. If you're using Scrum the rough structure of your Sprints will start to become visible, as product features are divided into the core functionality that needs to be delivered in early Sprints and extras that will be added to later builds. Constant communication with the end users will make this process much more effective in terms of delivery – would they rather have 10 percent functionality in a month or 25 percent in three months? Once you know what they want you can schedule Sprints to deliver it.

You'll also start to see the outline of your testing plan. As the tasks you need to carry out become obvious you'll begin to get an idea of what testing will be needed to complete them. Again don't get drawn into too much detail at this point, but what you work out will still generate a lot of information that will come in useful when development begins.

User Stories

User stories are one of the key elements of development in Scrum and XP, and every other Agile methodology has something with a different name but a similar function. They're not complicated; a user story is simply a very high level definition of a requirement. They're usually one line and make a simple statement of what the finished software will do. Here's an example:

Sales staff can view a customer's previous orders

Some developers prefer to phrase things more formally:

As a sales representative I want to be able to view a customer's previous orders

Either way it's just a statement that outlines a function. It doesn't say how that functionality is to be delivered and it doesn't break it down into subsidiary tasks. If it starts to become a compound sentence it's probably time to think about breaking it down into two or more separate user stories:

WRONG
Sales staff can take orders and check against inventory levels

---

RIGHT
1. Sales staff can take orders
2. Sales staff can check inventory levels

Some user stories are too large to be implemented in a single iteration. These are often called "epics," and they usually need to be broken down into a series of smaller stories. This tends to happen when they've worked their way nearly to the top of the priority stack, because there's no point in spending time on something that might never make it into the finished software.

User stories can often be organized into themes. Typical themes might be sales, stock control or access management. Themes can be used in several ways. You might want to allocate each theme to a planned release, or give one to each team to develop.

Where do user stories come from? One of the most common mistakes is for the developers to start writing them. That's missing the point – and also ignoring what the name implies. User stories need to be written by the stakeholders to ensure they're an accurate reflection of what the software will have to do. They also act as reminders to keep in touch with the shareholders throughout the project.

From the tester's point of view user stories give the rough outline of what needs to be tested. They don't give enough detail to start writing any actual testing code but they do serve as a heads up for what will be required later. That means testing begins as soon as user stories start coming in. The first step is making sure the stories are the size they should be and, if not, breaking them down until they are. This is a great point for testers to start building relationships with the stakeholders. Work with them as they write their user stories; if a story is taking too long start asking questions, find out what the stakeholder really wants and help express it simply.

It's important to look at user stories at the acceptance testing level. The story is going to say *As a user I need to be able to do X*. As a tester you need to visualize what's needed for X to be done, and discuss it with the stakeholder. If someone's going to be entering customer details into a form, what details are required? Which will be recordable but optional? Do any of the details need to be validated during the entry process and, if so, how? This will give you a list of pass/fail points that need to be passed before the software is delivered, and that's what you need to start working on your testing plan.

A common acronym used to describe a good user story is INVEST. Here it is:

I – Independent. Each user story has to stand on its own. This makes life easier when you start assigning tasks to sprints.

N – Negotiable. None of this is set in stone. Everyone is free to discuss alterations.

V – Valuable. A user story has to add value to someone. It may be value for the customer. It could also be value for the team. If you can't state what value it adds, however, what's it doing in the stack?

E – Estimable. You should be able to make a rough estimate – not a precise one, at this stage – of how long it should take to complete the work required by the story.

S – Small. Big stories aren't helpful. Split them down into small ones that let you identify and allocate discrete tasks.

T – <u>Testable</u>. User stories are requirements that you will be basing work on, so you need to be able to test them. Make sure they define clear, objective targets that can be verified through testing.

As a tester you have to make sure all these criteria – not just the last one – are met. If they are, the user story will add value to the project. If not, it won't help you and could even get in the way.

Testing Plan

With your user stories collected you're now in a position to start planning how you're going to test your project as it's developed. Of course the question is going to be asked – do you actually need to develop a test plan? Some Agile advocates argue against it, and suggest that a test plan is a holdover from the waterfall development method. The argument is that the test plan will generate itself throughout the development process:

• Before each sprint the contents of the release are discussed, letting the testers know what will need testing.

• Review of estimates lets the testers know the timescale for each feature, including how long it should take to test it.

• The testers will be involved in the "story writing" stage of each feature, when details are worked out, so they will already be working on testing scenarios.

• Once the sprint begins the testers are constantly working on new code as it's written. Short-term test planning is developed based on the day's activity and is a dynamic process.

According to this school of thought the effort that goes into creating a test plan would be better spent on developing better test scenarios, because these are what's actually going to identify defects in the software. This is correct – to a point. It certainly isn't a good idea to write a test plan that covers every last detail of what will be tested during the project, and how. There's nothing Agile about doing that; it doesn't only lock testers into a preplanned sequence, it constrains the code writers because they have to write what's due to be tested instead of what needs to be done.

On the other hand good Agile testing doesn't just follow on after the developers and check how well they've done their jobs; it's a key part of the overall work cycle. If you're doing Test Driven Development you need to know where to start writing tests. Your test plan is also going to cover the resources you need for the project. If you can be sure ahead of time that you'll need new software tools or even hardware to run all the required tests then get them arranged early; if there are delays in getting hold of them when they're needed that can hold up the entire project.

The nature of Agile means that each Sprint, iteration or Kanban task is going to need its own dedicated test plan, but you'll get the most out of your resources by having an overarching plan for the whole project. This should be developed during the release planning stage and typically it needs to take care of the following points:

- Scope of testing
- New functionalities to be tested
- Types and levels of testing
- Performance and load testing
- Testing infrastructure – environment, hardware and software
- Risk mitigation plan
- Resourcing
- Milestones and deliverables

In Agile methodologies everyone is involved in testing to some extent, including the customer. Developing the testing plan isn't a parallel activity stream; it's part of the core business of the whole team and everyone should be contributing to the plan.

There are five principles to keep in mind when you're laying out your testing plan:

- Test as **early as possible**. Most of the time the impact of a bug rises exponentially as time passes. Test Driven Development is the gold standard here.

- Test as **often as possible**. More frequent testing means a better chance of finding defects. Running more tests does increase short-term costs, but research shows that early and extensive investment in testing brings down total cost of ownership.

- Do **just enough** testing to meet project needs. Tests that are appropriate for a large financial system are overkill for a small journal's mailing list, and will achieve nothing beyond slowing down the project and pushing up costs. Don't gold-plate.

- Use **pair testing**. Testers work more effectively when they back each other up. Having a partner working with you makes it much less likely anything will be overlooked; one tests, the second immediately checks the results. Roles can be static or flexible – one tester and one developer, or two developers who swing between roles.

- Stay **flexible**. The test plan is a means, not an end. As the project develops elements of the plan might not fit how it's going. Be ready and willing to change things as required; don't stick to the plan just because it's The Plan.

The last principle is one that often falls by the wayside. When everyone's under pressure it's too easy to just fall back on The Plan. That's not Agile. It's also not efficient. It might *seem* like it's saving time and effort, but it isn't really. Trying to bend the project to fit an existing plan usually means you're just going to have to go back and redo it, generally because the plan didn't account for evolving requirements.

Development And Testing

It's once the development starts – whether it's the first Sprint in a Scrum project, or when the first batch of tasks moves to the "In progress" column on your Kanban chart – that testing really gets under way. Let's take the Scrum methodology as an example.

At the beginning of each Sprint there's a Sprint planning meeting. This usually lasts less than a day and lets the team make a number of key decisions for the upcoming work cycle:

• Review the Product Backlog and decide which items will be on the Sprint Backlog

• Outline the Sprint Backlog and make time estimates for each task

• Identify how much of the work can realistically be done during this Sprint

• Finalize the Sprint Backlog

Once the Sprint Backlog is confirmed developers will have a list of discrete tasks to be completed. Suitable test cases will be needed for each task, and if you're using Test Driven Development (TDD) those will be what you write first. It's vital to get them right.

Test Driven Development

Because most Agile development is carried out using TDD it's worth looking at in a bit more detail here. Using TDD, the team working on each item from the Backlog begins by planning what they want to do, deciding how to test it then writing the test. The process works like this:

1.   **Define the task.** If you don't know exactly what you're trying to do, you can't test to see if you've done it.

2.   **Write a test.** It should be a small one – it only has to test for the new feature.

3.   **Run the test.** Run the existing code (unless this is the first Sprint) through the new test and all the existing ones. It should pass all the tests except the new one, which it should fail. If it *doesn't* fail it that means the feature is already in the code or – more likely – the new test isn't working. Check and fix.

4.   **Write some code.** Write just enough code to implement the new feature. Keep it minimal; all you're trying to do is pass the test. Don't start gold-plating and adding extra functionality.

5.   **Run the tests again.** See if the expanded code passes the new test this time. If

it doesn't, fix it and try again. If it does, move on.

6.   **Refactor the code.** When the code is written the only objective is to pass the test. It doesn't matter if it doesn't do it in an elegant way; a pass is all that matters. Refactoring lets you clean up the code once you know it works.

7.   **Test again.** Repeat until the code passes all tests and is at an acceptable standard for release.

8.   **Define a new task.** Once that feature is satisfactory, take a new one from the Sprint Backlog or Work in Progress column and begin the process again.

This process is a great example of the iterative nature of Agile development. Instead of trying to write large sections of code then test and debug it all – usually a major task, and often a frustrating one – developers are always working with code that's almost all functional. If the code fails a test the failure will be in the small section that was just added, because everything else has already passed multiple runs. This makes identifying and fixing problems much easier because you know exactly where to look for them. Contrast that to the traditional approach, where it usually takes more time to find a bug than it does to fix it.

Testing Automation

Agile methodologies involve a lot of testing, so to minimize time and cost it's best to automate as much of it as possible. Some of the QA you need to do isn't suitable for automation but much of it is, and you should work out at an early stage what you can successfully automate. This matrix can help you decide where to direct your efforts:

Phase	Task	Can Automate?
Iteration Zero	Requirements	No
	Design	No
Implementation	Code Review	Yes
	Unit Testing	Yes
	Integration Testing	Yes
	User Acceptance Testing	No
Delivery	Post-delivery bugs	No

Timeboxing

Although you're trying to avoid inflexible planning it's still essential to keep track of progress, and to ensure that user stories aren't taking longer to complete than they should be. Timeboxing is a common method used by Agile teams to keep things running to the overall project schedule without becoming excessively rigid. At the start of each iteration the Sprint backlog and estimated time have already been decided. If timings start to slip, however, there are two ways to proceed. Firstly, aim to fulfil the entire Sprint backlog but stretch the timescale; secondly, timebox the problem – aim to deliver a lower-featured but still working piece of software in the original timescale. Testers play a key role in advising this decision. If the delay looks like being minor it may save time overall to let a slight slip occur now, and avoid adding another Sprint later. On the other hand a particularly sticky problem could create a major bottleneck and leave timeboxing as the best solution. In an Agile environment testers need to be willing to do a lot more than just verify that code runs.

Obviously timeboxing isn't the ideal outcome of a Sprint, but if the rest of the project can proceed with what's actually been produced then the extra backlog can be worked in later; it's preferable to having the rest of the team sit around while that one piece of the job is finished.

Types Of Testing

Testing is split into several sub-categories, carried out at different points during an iteration. These are often depicted as the Agile testing quadrants:

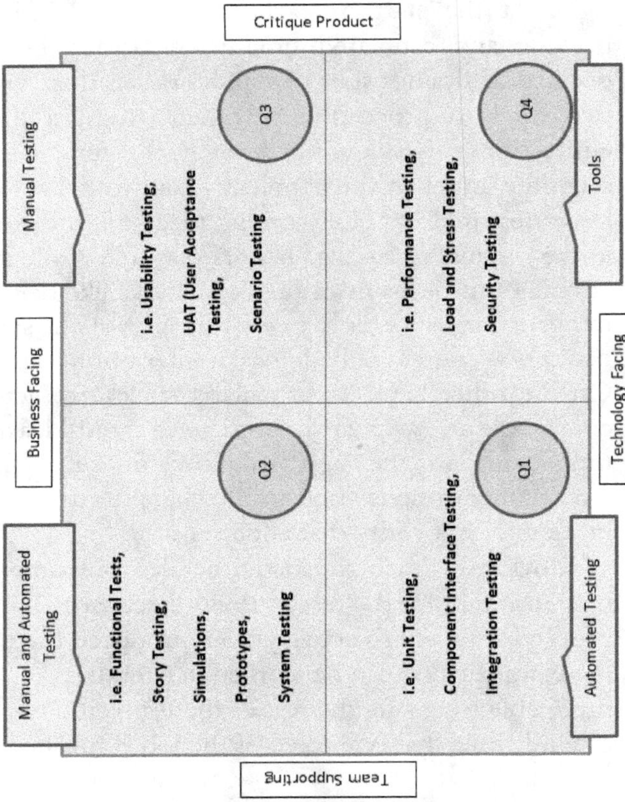
Critique Product
Manual Testing
Business Facing
Manual and Automated Testing
i.e. Usability Testing,
UAT (User Acceptance Testing,
Scenario Testing
Q3
i.e. Functional Tests,
Story Testing,
Simulations,
Prototypes,
System Testing
Q2
i.e. Performance Testing,
Load and Stress Testing,
Security Testing
Q4
Tools
Technology Facing
i.e. Unit Testing,
Component Interface Testing,
Integration Testing
Q1
Automated Testing
Team Supporting

(see http://www.agile-testing.com/ebook-illustrations for a higher resolution)

There's no particular order to run the tests in each quadrant, and in fact tests can even be moved between quadrants if that fits what's required. If a unit test meets a requirement that's business-facing and supports the team it's in Quadrant 2. Flexibility, as usual, is the key.

This figure shows the full range of potential tests that may be carried out, but the standard list is somewhat shorter:

Unit Testing

As soon as the Sprint Backlog has been decided the testing effort begins. The first level is unit testing – verifying the software every time code is added, to make sure it has the right functionality and no bugs have been introduced. This is usually carried out by the developers themselves and is TDD-based.

Unit testing should be a more or less constant activity during the sprint. Every time code is added, run the tests. At the end of each day, run the tests. Think a feature is completed? Run the tests again. This is where many people familiar with traditional development get uncomfortable with Agile. Is all this testing really necessary? Isn't it wasting time and increasing costs? The answer to that is a clear "No!" It needs to be stressed that finding issues early *saves* time and money. The longer a bug remains in the code the more work will be needed to remedy it once it's identified.

How much testing is enough? That's where acceptance criteria come in. Developing these is part of user acceptance testing (AUT) and we'll look at it in more detail there, but the key point is that the code has to do what the customer wants. If it's running flawlessly but the functionality it provides doesn't match what's needed it isn't acceptable. That's why user input is vital for developing the right tests.

Integration Testing

Unless your project is a small, simple one the chances are you're going to have to carry out integration testing as well as unit testing. Are there multiple teams, each working on a part of the final product? Have you used branching to solve a problem and now you're bringing multiple versions back into the main codeline? Then integration testing is going to be required. The unit testing process will ensure that each component is bug-free and performing to specification, but that doesn't say anything about how they will work together. Before the software is delivered you need to be sure that each component can communicate with the others as required, and that nothing has any adverse effects on anything else.

There are two ways to do this. The traditional approach is to complete and test all the components, then integrate them and test the full system. If any tests are failed the QA team will then isolate the problem and pass the affected components back to the developers to solve it.

The Agile approach is very different, and closely mirrors the unit testing process. Integration testing should be run early and often. The ideal is to use a daily or continuous build for testing, which should preferably be automated. Here is the ideal process for achieving that:

A new or updated piece of code is tested and checked out. Once it's met the acceptance criteria it is added to the project code base to be built. The build combines all the existing code into an application. At this stage some QA has already been done – you've verified that all the code fits together without breaking the build. Once a component is built it should still be able to pass all the tests it passed to get signed off. However this doesn't tell you how well it can interact with the other components.

To verify function the integration tests need to be run on the build. Your aim is to test whether or not all the components work together to produce the required result, so it's critical that you develop test cases that will validate that. You can choose to do this as a separate task, component interface testing.

Component Interface Testing

Component interface testing is often counted as a subset of integration testing, but in many teams it's seen as important enough to be classed separately. Whether you see it as a separate test program or not it's definitely something that needs attention. Almost any project is going to involve data passing back and forth between components of the software and, especially where components have been developed by different teams, it's essential to verify that it's happening the way it should.

Many developers are skeptical of the ability to test components before they're integrated; as the components of the software are designed to work together, they think, how can they be tested in isolation? That's where interfaces come in. Each component interacts with the others through interfaces, which is basically any feature of the component that handles data going in or out. Let's take an example; a component for an academic database application that handles student access to various data repositories. The component can be treated as a black box, like this:

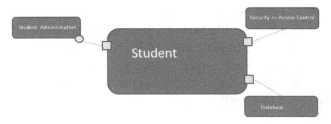

(see http://www.agile-testing.com/ebook-illustrations for a higher resolution)

Each of the three squares around the border is an interface, where the component interacts with others. Now, even if the student administration component isn't available you can still test that interface. When the component receives a security validation request from a database (lower right interface) it should call up the student administration component through the left interface. To test this, all you have to do is check that it's calling the student administration component in the correct format. You don't need the student administration component itself there to receive the call; you just need something that will fail if the call isn't correctly implemented.

Integration testing is a great way to encourage developers to stick to industry standards. Tweaking things isn't as tempting when it means they're going to have to write a new test to verify the data a component is sending or receiving, instead of using a standard one.

Integration testing can throw up unexpected results, but it's likely to go a lot more smoothly if each run begins with all the components able to talk to each other. That way you'll be able to isolate the source of a bug much more quickly, as well as confirming what *does* work as intended.

System Testing

The system testing stage can be compared to the point in the waterfall process where most of the testing occurs. You've planned the project, developed all the components and integrated them into a complete system. Each component is sending and receiving data the way it's supposed to. Now you have to make sure that the system delivers the functionality that the customer is looking for. Typically that's done as a major testing effort towards the end of the process. The testing team has a list of tasks the software needs to carry out, and it will be tested against those tasks to verify how well it does them.

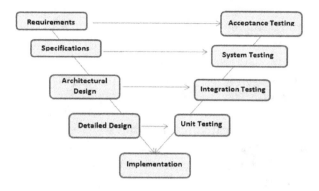

(see http://www.agile-testing.com/ebook-illustrations for a higher resolution)

Being Agile, you've started developing ways to test the specifications as soon as they firmed up. That should have begun in Iteration 0 but of course it's a process that's continuously developed and refined as the project runs. Agile development doesn't emphasize highly detailed specifications at the start, so in the initial Sprints the pass criteria can be quite broad. As the system takes shape and specifications become tighter new test cases will be written to stay on track. You often won't have a good enough idea of the specifications to write a test until the Sprint planning – or even the Sprint itself – gets under way.

Through your project testing has been done routinely by the developers themselves, and if you've implemented TDD correctly it's been the engine that's driven the writing of code. Even if you've had dedicated testers they should have been working closely with the development team at every stage. At the system testing level, however, there are strong arguments in favor of having a dedicated testing team to carry out much of the work. It's not essential to do it that way but it does have benefits that might match your project.

Using the waterfall model the test team is usually independent of the developers – often it's even in a separate division of the organization. The justification for that is that the testers are able to locate and report faults without pressure from the lead developers. That doesn't work in an Agile environment. As soon as you create an air gap between developers and testers you start to build in delays and communication problems.

The benefit of using a dedicated test team is the extra expertise and resources it can throw at testing. To get the most out of that it's essential that the testers continue to work directly with the developers. That way they can immediately pass bugs to the people who can fix them, and even give advice on what needs done. If there's an air gap between the two you'll start to move back towards the delivery of traditional detailed bug lists, and that needs to be avoided – it's just a source of delay.

Performance, Load And Stress Testing

Sometimes considered as part of system testing, this is required to make sure the software can handle the actual conditions it will be working under. A component might pass all the tests when it's handling one call, but how will it do when it's handling 1,000 calls a second? It's important to check with a realistic load, and while that's a distraction for the developers it's the sort of task the quality assurance team is there to carry out. As far as possible the software should be tested in an environment that matches the one it will be used in, including multiple browsers and operating systems if necessary.

User Acceptance Testing

User Acceptance Testing (UAT) is a process aimed at confirming the software meets the requirements mutually agreed on by developers and customers. It verifies that the system performs the required business functions in a way that's acceptable to the end users.

In a waterfall project UAT happens at the end of the process. The software has been designed, built, tested and integrated; now it's all tested again to make sure the final product meets the client's needs. Usually the client is involved in this testing, for the obvious reason, but sometimes they simply supply a detailed list of requirements and the final build is tested against them. There are some major potential drawbacks to this method, however. If defects are found at such a late stage fixing them is likely to seriously delay delivery of the project; it's much cheaper and faster to fix them earlier in the process. There's also the risk that what's been developed isn't exactly what the customer was looking for.

Of course the principle behind this method is obvious; build it then test it. The Agile system of UAT seems, at first, a lot less intuitive – it kicks in right at the beginning of the project, long before there's anything for the users to accept. In fact it makes a lot of sense to do it this way, because the risks at later stages will be massively reduced. Consider how much effort is wasted when the customer sees the finished software and says "No, I don't want it to do it this way." At best a user interface redesign might be needed; at worst the whole system will need a major overhaul. Doing it the Agile way avoids this scenario. Early in the Sprint a developer will put together a minimal version of a possible solution and ask the customer, "Will something like this do?" If they say no, the developer will try something else and ask again. If they say yes, the team can get to work on developing the demonstrator into working software. That's user acceptance testing and it can happen very early in the project – even during Iteration 0. Once the initial brainstorming session has come up with a proposed architecture, just ask the client if it matches their requirements.

The same principles should be followed throughout the project. If UAT is a constant, ongoing process there shouldn't be any unwelcome surprises right before release. So how should it be scheduled and implemented?

• The bulk of UAT should be done during regular sprints. During Iteration 0 each Scrum Master (or the equivalent in other Agile methodologies) creates UAT User Stories for their area of the project. These are then firmed up and divided into sub-tasks that can be tested. It's vital for end users to be involved at this stage, to make sure the tasks accurately reflect what the user is looking for. The tests are written and run during the Sprint until the code passes each one. At that point the User Story can be closed and laid aside for later use.

• Final UAT is run during Stabilization Sprints. Stabilization Sprints are the last stage before a product release and no new code should be written during them. Their main purpose is to isolate and deal with bugs that have been introduced during system integration and managed to get past integration testing. The UAT element of these sprints is conducted by subject matter experts and product owners. This is where the UAT done during the regular sprints pays off; it's likely the users will suggest tweaks and refinements, but highly *un*likely that any major changes will be required – they will have been picked up and resolved much earlier in the project.

If UAT is done thoroughly throughout the project cycle you should reach the Stabilization Sprint with all major bugs, and features that don't conform to user stories, already rectified.

Delivery

The whole point of the development process is to get working software into the hands of the users. Waterfall and Agile processes go about that in different ways, but the end result is the same (or should be). The iterative nature of Agile development has several implications for how you should actually go about delivering it, though.

A key principle of Agile development is that each iteration should result in working software, even if it doesn't yet have all the functionality of the final product. This is a huge strength of Agile, but it also presents its own challenges. The main one is in deciding how the software should actually be delivered. Are you going to ship limited but functional versions as they're available, or wait until the product is complete? There are several factors that can affect that decision, with one of the main ones being what the end user wants.

If the iterations have been properly planned the core functionality should have been produced first. Some clients may prefer to have the software delivered in a form that meets their most urgent requirements, then incrementally add more functionality as it's developed. This usually depends on the client's own corporate culture and structure, as well as the specific circumstances around this release. Larger organizations with a more formalized procurement system are likely to prefer a single, well documented handover than a series of upgrades.

Planning how to test during the release iteration depends on several factors. One of them that's often not as much under your control as you would like is how the project reaches the end game. Ideally it will be coming in on schedule and under budget, with the defect rate down to a level that's acceptable to all stakeholders. If you're using Scrum a common tactic is to run a burn-down chart showing what's left in the requirements stack, with an agreed list of items that need to be cleared before delivery.

Unfortunately it's also not unheard of that you need to deliver because your hand is being forced. There are two common scenarios for that:

- You're coming up to a non-negotiable delivery date and it's taking longer to clear the bug list than you had expected. There are various reasons why the delivery date might be set in stone – the most likely is that it's written into the contract and the buyer isn't willing to extend. Most developers would much rather deliver solid software late than a buggy product on time, but either through inflexibility or urgent need the client may insist on delivery by the deadline.

- The project may have hit its budget limit, and the client has stopped funding further development and requested delivery of the current build. If this happens you're going to have to deploy the software as it was at the end of the last finished iteration.

Obviously neither of these situations is ideal, but using an Agile methodology means that when they do arise you're in a much stronger position than you would be if you'd stuck to the waterfall system. Because Agile aims to have working software at the end of each iteration you're much more likely to have something that's production-ready and can be handed over, but it's not a situation any team wants to experience.

Whether the end of the project is running to schedule or not, it's going to need careful attention to testing. Agile experts will tell you that the release iteration is not a testing phase, and they're right. The bulk of the real testing will have been done throughout development, as we've already discussed. Some more is still going to be needed though.

During each construction iteration, as well as adding new functionality the developers will have been identifying and fixing bugs left from the previous one. At the end of the final construction iteration all the code that's going to be in the release is there, but so are whatever faults managed to slip through. Part of the tester's job during the release iteration is to find and fix them, as shown:

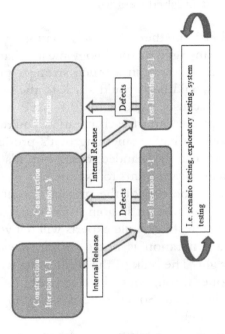

(see http://www.agile-testing.com/ebook-illustrations for a higher resolution)

At this point the testers aren't doing TDD; they're simply running all their function tests to verify that the software does what it's supposed to. Any bugs that are found should go straight back to the developers to be fixed, but no new code is being added in this iteration.

There are different strategies for doing the actual handover of the software. The customer may want to put it straight into operation. On the other hand they might want to run a beta phase with a subset of the end users, to identify any remaining issues. If you've managed to keep stakeholders involved through the development process it should be possible to cut this stage down or even eliminate it completely; the software should be a close match for customer requirements and the extensive testing that's been done means the bug list at distribution should be short.

To ensure a successful deployment it's vital that you don't look at the software in isolation. Several external factors can affect how the delivery works out, and some preparatory work will often be needed to smooth the way. Here are some of the key points to consider:

• **Legacy systems**. It's almost inevitable that the new system will have to interact with legacy ones, whether it's joining them or replacing them. Don't rely on input/output specifications when ensuring compatibility, because even if you get the interfaces right they can still interact with your product in unexpected ways. Running versions of these systems with appropriate data need to be part of your testing environment.

• **Data conversion**. Will the system be working with legacy data? If so there's a good chance some or all of that data will need to be converted into a format the software can work with. That needs to be factored in early in the development process and you'll need test cases to verify your conversion system.

• **User environment**. It's disturbingly common for clients to order new software without making sure their existing IT infrastructure can run it. Finding out there are problems just before delivery can lead to delays or extra costs. Work with stakeholders to ensure the systems are in place to operate the product. Evaluate hardware, operating systems, network architecture and databases.

• **Training**. Make sure you know exactly what the training requirements are. Obviously the end users will need to be trained to use your software, but is that all? Will they also need to learn a new operating system or database application? Strictly speaking it might not be your responsibility to handle these requirements, but you'll get the blame if it isn't done.

• **Documentation**. You'll need to supply supporting documentation along with the software. At a minimum this is going to involve manuals for users and support staff, but there may be more extensive requirements. Manuals need tested too – check every instruction they contain to see what happens.

There are also straight technical issues to be considered. The software has to be installed on the client's systems, and that means you need installation scripts. You'll get Agile benefits of you develop these in parallel with the software itself; the software can act as its own test case and you'll end each iteration with a product that can be installed if required. If you're looking for a good model for how to do this, a good start is to use your installer to move the latest build from your development sandbox to the test environment. If you're managing to do that successfully every time you run tests you'll be building a solid foundation for getting the finished product into service with the end users.

Don't neglect the worst-case scenario, either. What if, despite all your QA efforts, an unforeseen problem occurs during installation or you have to roll back the project for some other reason? Make sure you have a de-installation script ready to go as well, just in case you have to back off from deployment once you're already working on it. Once again this script needs to be thoroughly tested to minimize the risk if it ever needs to be implemented.

Implementation

Hopefully by now you can see the value of Agile as a philosophy for software development, so now how do you put it into practice? The good news is that it doesn't mean tearing your entire system apart and starting again. Agile can be implemented incrementally, and can even be added to an existing waterfall project. The key to that is the use of hybrid systems – a mix of the most appropriate parts of traditional and Agile practices.

The Value Of Hybrid Systems

So far we've mostly looked at Agile methods as a direct replacement for the traditional waterfall process. In reality most projects use a hybrid of the two. This makes perfect sense – there are areas where waterfall has advantages, after all. It can also be easier to sell Agile to management as an add-on to existing processes rather than as a replacement for them. As an example let's take SAP ERP.

SAP ERP is one of the leading frameworks for enterprise resource planning, and can deliver major benefits to an organization that manages to implement it successfully. Its suite of modules integrates well, sidestepping many of the commonly encountered problems involved in integrating components from multiple suppliers.

However implementing SAP ERP can be a risky process. Failures to plan the transition to SAP are a common cause of project failure, as are inadequate testing and training. Even delays in completing the implementation result in a loss of value from the investment that's been sunk into the software. That means it's vital to choose the correct methodology to see your SAP implementation through.

Many IT professionals believe that Agile isn't well suited to an SAP implementation and that the (perceived) greater clarity of a waterfall approach will deliver better results. SAP themselves don't agree – they have switched to Agile for much of their software development. Depending on the culture of your own organization Agile can be a perfect match for SAP, but you're also likely to face a lot of resistance.

A common perception is that ERP projects are too complex to fit well with Agile. This is based on the widespread belief that Agile works best for small tasks that can be easily implemented in a single iteration, and scales poorly to larger projects. In particular Agile is seen as lacking the control and coordination needed to manage the large number of dependencies in a SAP ERP implementation. What worries IT managers is that studies show a number of common failure points for SAP rollouts:

- Lack of robust processes
- Lack of robust tools
- Lack of documentation
- Lack of detailed planning

Managers without experience of Agile believe that these are areas devalued by the Agile philosophy, leading to an increased risk of failure. In fact to a limited extent they're right – documentation, for example, definitely *is* devalued in Agile. In other respects they're wrong. A good Agile team *will* have robust tools and processes and it *will* carry out adequate planning. What it won't do is apply those tools and processes rigidly, or plan to a level of detail that exceeds their ability to see into the future.

Arguments For Waterfall
- Potentially more acceptable to senior decision makers – clearer process
- Extensive documentation of requirements and implementation timetable
- Overarching plan

Arguments For Agile

- Earlier delivery of core functionality (leading to earlier return on investment)
- Reduced risk of delivered software not meeting user requirements
- Costs and delivered value of each Sprint are clearly identified
- Training needs are identified early
- Extensive, ongoing testing pinpoints required legacy system upgrades

The fact is that Agile can be scaled up to cope with a large project like SAP implementation very successfully, and there are many cases where it's a much lower-risk strategy than the waterfall process. When a new project is in the planning stage look at the tasks and risks involved and assess whether they're straightforward enough to be run through waterfall development or if Agile will give you the flexibility you need to get the job done quicker.

Conclusion

Agile testing has been in use for over a decade now and despite some resistance it's come to be accepted as a mainstream development technique. It's not likely that will change in the future. Software was once a commodity, something that people bought in a box and used until a new product was released. That's all changed now. With software increasingly downloaded from the internet and patched regularly, the iterative nature of Agile is the best – possibly the only – solution for computer users who want to keep everything up to date. From fixing security bugs in a corporate data management system to tweaking your smartphone apps for better performance, everyone is now used to continuous development and software that's never really "finished". The Agile philosophy could have been tailor-made for today's software market and looks strongly placed to become even more widespread. Any possible replacement will have to use the same basic principles; a return to the linear principle of the waterfall method isn't a realistic option at this point.

So what does that mean for your own project? It means that Agile is an approach you have to at least consider, and for most projects you'll probably get better results if you apply at least some Agile principles during development.

Despite skepticism from some developers – usually in large, established organizations - Agile can be easily scaled to suit any size of project, even very complex ones involving multiple development teams. The key to scaling is to be flexible – take time before development starts to consider how you see the project progressing, look for potential bottlenecks or conflict points and consider adding elements of the waterfall method where they can help. As we saw in the case of SAP projects there are times when a combination of the two systems will give the best results, so don't be afraid to mix and match where appropriate.

Even once you've made the decision to go Agile it can be hard to unlearn old practices. A common error is to divide a project into sprints, but then to view each sprint as a mini-waterfall. That's missing the point of Agile – real iterative development depends on the test-code-validate-refactor process we've covered.

Glossary

Acceptance Criteria – The benchmarks used to judge whether a work item or user story has been completed. These criteria are usually all or nothing – for the item to be completed every criteria must be passed.

Acceptance Test Driven Development (ATDD) – A process where the team agree on *acceptance criteria* before beginning work, then create the tests necessary to verify those criteria, with development of the actual software being the last task.

Acceptance Testing – The process used to verify that *acceptance criteria* have been met. In most Agile teams this is done using automated tests wherever possible.

Agile SCM Tool – A Software Configuration Management tool suitable for use with Agile development methods.

Backlog – A backlog is a prioritized list of tasks to be achieved. It can include user stories or identified defects that must be fixed.

Branching – This is a way to try out multiple solutions by duplicating an object (like a piece of code or a directory tree) and allowing the two versions to be developed independently. Merging support is used so code changes made on each branch can be integrated later.

Burndown Chart – This is a graphic representation of how much is left to be done on a project. It's usually drawn as a chart that shows work remaining on the X axis and time elapsed on Y.

Burnup Chart – An alternative to a *Burndown Chart*, this shows the number of user stories completed.

Change and Configuration Management – This is the software-based process that tracks the progress of a project. It covers version control, branching and merging, issue tracking and other technical aspects.

Continuous Integration – A keystone of Agile, this is the system where each change to the code is integrated into the main line as soon as possible. Doing so means problems can be identified and resolved more quickly.

Cross-Functional Team – A team whose members have all the skills and specialties necessary to complete a project.

Distributed Development - Development working on the same project but located across worksites.

Epic - A *user story* covering a wide range of requirements, which is then broken down into a number of smaller stories.

Hybrid Process - Development process that uses both Agile and non-Agile practices together.

Iteration – The basic Agile work cycle, aimed at delivering a part of the overall project as working software.

Kanban – Agile development system based on Lean practices and using a visual work tracking system – the Kanban board.

One Piece Flow - A process in which each developer works on one piece at a time; pieces are then pulled downstream to the next process.

Pair Programming – A continuous review process where two developers work at one station; one writes code and the other reviews it line by line in real time.

Product Backlog - The backlog owned by the Product Owner.

Refactoring – Continuously improving the usability and reliability of code without changing its behavior. Refactoring results in more adaptable code and is well suited to an iterative development process.

Release Management - Release management comprises activities aimed at ensuring that software is ready to be released to customers.

Release Process – The final stage in development, where the software has been verified and is handed over to the customer.

Scrum – An Agile method based around Sprints. The team usually consists of a Product Owner, Scrum Master and Scrum team.

Scrum Master – Someone who facilitates Scrum meetings, manages resource allocation and tracks Scrum team progress.

Software Configuration Management (SCM) – A system put in place to store, track and release versions of a product. Usually implemented through tracking software.

Sprint Backlog – The features the team plan to implement during the upcoming Sprint.

Sprint Review – A washup carried out after an iteration in which teams go over and demonstrate the backlog items they covered during it.

Stand-up – A short, *Timeboxed* daily meeting where obstacle can be discussed and hopefully quickly resolved.

Story Points - Relative effort required by a team to implement a user story. More challenging stories have more points. This can be used to measure *Velocity*.

Task Board - A physical or electronic board representing the state of tasks in a current iteration. The Kanban board is a classic example.

Test Driven Development (TDD) – A software development process where the test is written first and the code incrementally improved until it passes the test.

Timeboxing – A practice where activities are allocated a specific amount of time. It can be applied to development iterations, meetings or almost anything else.

Unit Testing - Tests applied to small sections of functionality.

User Story - An Agile method for defining user requirements; usually given as a simple statement that can be fitted on a 3x5 index card.

Velocity – A team's rate of progress through the backlog, often measured by the number of *Story Points* they complete each week.

Waterfall – Traditional software development model where progress is measured through a number of predefined and linear stages.

XP - "Extreme Programming," an Agile implementation that emphasizes using the simplest possible code, using practices such as pair programming, incremental design and continuous integration.

Index

www.ingramcontent.com/pod-product-compliance
Lightning Source LLC
Chambersburg PA
CBHW061015050326
40689CB00012B/2648